THIS BOOK BELONGS TO

....

ISBN: 978-1-78324-295-5

Book design by Wordzworth
www.wordzworth.com

The Story of

SAMMY & ZELDA

by

Susan McCray &
Stan Ivar Abrahamsen

Illustrated by
David Calabrese

I dedicate this book to Franceska, Harry, and Kent.
Whenever I felt lost, each were able to find me with love
understanding and generosity. All who knew them loved
them as I did. All who didn't know them wish they had.

—SUSAN McCRAY—

I dedicate this book to my parents, Stanley & Ingrid
the first to introduce and teach my brother Peter
and I about boats, the sea and all her endless wonders.

To Capt. Dan Salas of Harbor Breeze Cruises for allowing
me to skipper the Kristina for over twenty plus years.

and my 1st officer Scott Louie for your support.

To my good friend, and now fellow author, Susan McCray, for without
whom this wonderful story would never have been written down

To my new friend David and his exceptionally beautiful artwork
bringing it all to life. And to all the beautiful sea lions
of the oceans, especially my two favorites,
Sammy and Zelda forever playing and snoozing on buoy #2.

—STAN IVAR ABRAHAMSEN—

Captain Stan with his first mate Louie stood at the boarding entrance ramp of the tour boat Kristina and warmly greeted all the passengers who would cruise with them today.

Once everyone was on board, Captain Stan and Louie moved to the boat's wheelhouse, and announced over the Public Address system, "Welcome aboard the Kristina everyone, it is so great to have you with us. Please watch your step as you walk around the boat. A special message for all the children, there's no running or jumping or standing on the seats. Is everyone ready? Then here we go!"

Captain Stan reaches for the lever and Kristina's loud horn bellows to all the other boats as it moves from Rainbow Harbor and heads out to sea.

3

As the Kristina makes its first turn, Captain Stan announces to the passengers, "I'd like to introduce you to some of my very best friends. To your right, sitting and lying on the red buoy with Number 2 at the top, are two sea lions, Sammy and Zelda. Sitting on top of Zelda's straw hat is Sydney Seagull and sitting on Sammy's blue cap is Roofus Seagull. As you look to your left there's my friend Tiny the whale. Sammy and Zelda spend a lot of time together and with their friends."

Sammy and Zelda enjoyed sleeping on the buoy in the
harbor but today they are having a disagreement.
Zelda wanted to sleep, and Sammy kept waking her up.

Zelda finally said, "I'm trying to sleep Sammy, stop waking me up!"

6

After several times of telling Sammy to stop waking her up Zelda
decided to swim to shore and once there, she waddled from Shoreline
Village to Ocean Boulevard in search of a quiet place to rest.

Zelda was not very familiar with the streets and got stuck in the middle of an intersection. Horns honked and traffic swerved to avoid hitting her. Bystanders waved traffic to go around her. From their truck, two men took sawhorses to block traffic, and green netting to safeguard Zelda. A little dog named Scruffy stopped cars by barking and ran circles around Zelda to protect her.

8

Angela, who worked at the Sand 'n' Sea Candy Store,
looked out the store window and worried about all the traffic
headed Zelda's way. The little dog Scruffy continued to
shield Zelda from the dangerous, oncoming traffic.

Meanwhile, back out on the big red buoy, Sammy was really worried
not knowing where Zelda was. Sammy decided to ask Sidney and
Roofus for help. He said, "Please help me find Zelda. Sidney, can you
go towards the town and Roofus can you fly out toward the ocean?"

"Don't worry," said Sidney.
"We will find her and bring her back. She must have gotten lost."

Both seagulls took off. As Sidney looked below at the land,
she spotted a little dog running around and barking.
A few feet away there was Zelda. Sidney flew
down and landed on Zelda's head.

12

"Zelda, what were you doing out there? Everyone was so worried
about you! Sammy sent me and Roofus out to find you.
Even Tiny was looking everywhere for you, Let's go!
Just follow me and I'll get you back to the ocean as fast as I can."

As Sidney and Zelda were about to leave, they looked back and saw little Scruffy standing by himself, watching them, feeling terribly sad to be left alone yet again. Scruffy had been in and out of animal shelters, left homeless on the streets, and on his own many times in the past.

Zelda looked at Sidney and said, "Are you thinking what I'm thinking?"

Sidney and Zelda both went over and asked Scruffy,
"Do you want to come back with us? We think Captain Stan
would love to have you with him on the boat."

16

Scruffy wagged his tail.
He was so delighted not to be left behind again.
"Oh yes, please, I'd love to follow you back," he barked.

Off they went. Sidney led the way, Zelda waddled behind him,
and Scruffy happily followed. The people on the street
waved and shouted good-bye. One father said to his children,
"Zelda left us with a lot of fond memories today."

Sammy saw all of them coming back towards
the boat and cried, "Zelda I was so worried!
Everyone was looking for you. What happened?"

Zelda explained, "When I saw all the traffic and people
I got lost and very frightened. I'm so thankful Sidney found me."

Sidney said, "You're welcome, Zelda.
We were all so worried about you.
I'm so glad I spotted Scruffy and heard him barking."

Sammy begged, "Please Zelda don't ever do this again."

She replied, "I won't Sammy, I promise. I'm sorry. "

Captain Stan greeted them and said, "We're all glad you're back Zelda."

Everyone on the boat applauded to demonstrate they all agreed with Captain Stan.

Captain Stan then looked down and
saw Scruffy looking up at him and asked, "Who is this little guy?"

Sidney replied, "This is Scruffy. He helped save Zelda from the street traffic.
Zelda and I hoped it was all right with you to have him come back with us."

Captain Stan looked at the little dog and asked, "Hi there Scruffy, do you like the ocean?"

Scruffy answered, "I sure do now!!!"

Captain Stan said, "I have an idea. I think Scruffy can be our guard
dog on the Kristina. What do you think of that everyone?"

Scruffy stood up looking very proud, stuck out his chest and barked
using his best voice, "I'd be grateful and proud to be of service sir."

Captain Stan looked at all the passengers and stated, "This is what I call
a happy ending." All on board the Kristina applauded in agreement.

21

Captain Stan spoke to everyone on the ship and said, "Thank you all for coming aboard the Kristina and meeting all my friends, especially my new one Scruffy. We all look forward to seeing you again!"

"Isn't that right Scruffy?" questioned Captain Stan.

Scruffy saluted with an "Aye, aye Captain Stan!"

Captain Stan saluted back, and then pulled the lever once again and sounded the loud boat horn to announce the Kristina's safe return to the harbor.

Author Susan McCray

The Story of Sammy and Zelda is Susan McCray's third children's book. She is the author of the delightfully whimsical Paddy Platypus and of the inspiring story Harry's Piano, based on the early life of her father, Academy Award Winning pianist, and composer Harry Sukman. She is currently producing an animated film based on the book.

As Vice President of Talent for Michael Landon Productions?, Ms. McCray was the casting director of many acclaimed episodic television series including Little House on the Prairie, Father Murphy, and Highway to Heaven. She also cast the television movies The Diary of Anne Frank, The Loneliest Runner and Where Pigeons Go to Die. In a career that spanned more than _____years, she cast numerous shows for NBC, CBS, and PBS.

As a producer, Ms. McCray's credits include the celebrated documentaries: Michael Landon: Memories of Laughter and Love; Remembering Kent McCray: Laughter Love and Television; and Don Collier: Confessions of an Acting Cowboy. She also produced the CD: Warm Heart Cool Hands, a compilation of some of her father's award-winning music. Currently, Ms. McCray is producing and hosting the podcast Kaleidoscope, airing on/at *mixcloud.com*, and through/on radio station KJEWL. She is also the creator and host of the syndicated radio feature Hollywood Hotline.

Susan McCray's humanitarian spirit embodies passionate support for her favorite charities. She frequently organizes, produces and serves as Mistress of Ceremonies for a variety of fundraising events, is currently an "advocate" for KidsPlay Children's Museum in Torrington, CT.

Stanley Ivar Abrahamsen

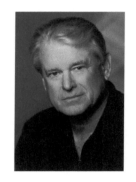

This is Stanley Ivar Abrahamsen's first children's book. Capt. Stan has been visiting with the real Sammy & Zelda for many years as captain on Harbor Breeze's tour boat Kristina.

A graduate of SUNY Maritime College at Fort Schuyler, he is a U.S. Merchant Marine Licensed Captain & Engineer. During Vietnam he served aboard various cargo ships delivering cargo to Vietnam ports while also fulfilling his military service obligation as a Lieutenant in the U.S. Navy.

Known professionally as 'Stan Ivar' within the entertainment industry he continues to have a successful acting career. Naturally his most memorable show is the one that gave him his start in Hollywood: "Little House on the Prairie."

Under the Child 5 Productions banner he and four other actors produced the Los Angeles Pro-Celebrity Charity Rodeos. All rodeo proceeds were distributed between four other separate children's charities and one individual needy child.

Stan always loves seeing and waving to Sammy & Zelda out on Bouy #2.

Smooth Sailing Kids!

25